© 2000 by Barbour Publishing, Inc.

ISBN 1-58660-784-7

Cover image © PhotoDisc, Inc.

Published by Humble Creek, P.O. Box 719, Uhrichsville, Ohio 44683

Printed in China.
5 4 3 2 1

EVERYDAY
Angels

SIMPLE WAYS TO BE AN ANGEL
FOR OTHERS EVERY DAY

Karon Phillips Goodman

HUMBLECREEK

INSPIRATION FOR LIFE

*Be completely humble and gentle;
be patient,
bearing with one another in love.*

EPHESIANS 4:2

INTRODUCTION

Do you know an angel? Maybe you know several. Do you want to be one? Maybe you've been an angel thousands of times. I'm sure you can remember times when angels reached out to you—not angels in the visionary, miraculous sense, but angels in the tangible, earthly sense. Those were *everyday angels.*

You know those people—the ones who have entered your life at good times and bad, who have been just the godsend that you needed right when you needed it. Maybe your angel was your spouse or your child or a friend or even a stranger. All of these people have probably been angels to you at one time or another, and when it happened, you counted yourself richly blessed.

No doubt, you've been someone's angel, too, when you shared and helped and guided and loved, or maybe just listened. Somehow, you knew just what to do to touch someone's life. You probably didn't think of yourself as an angel at the time, but that's exactly what angels do—touch peoples' lives and make a difference. And here's great news: You can do that every day.

Our lives are filled with stress and fear and disappointment. But the everyday angels get us through with that interaction that says, "I care—you're not alone." These simple acts of kindness often take no more than a few seconds, but they bind us together in a troubled world. They help us see beyond ourselves. They give us hope and joy. There is nothing more angelic than that.

You can be an angel every day—giving and sharing, and receiving blessing in the process. Everything you give comes back to you over and over. Try it and see, with the one hundred ways suggested in this book. They're just a smattering of the countless ways you can join the *Everyday Angels*.

CHAPTER 1

What Is an Angel?

We've all read of those angels that foretell historic events or deliver messages in dreams or protect believers from harm. They are immortal, supernatural, intangible—and quite scarce. They are angels of the heavenly kind, but they aren't the only kind of angels. Thankfully, we live in a world full of a far more common kind of angel, those everyday angels that are completely mortal yet undoubtedly spiritual, no less sent by God than those of Abraham's day.

An angel is sometimes defined as "a spiritual being" or "an attendant spirit." I like those definitions. They're easy to understand and not limited to the surreal angels of biblical lore. You and I are both "spiritual beings." The life God breathed into us is not only a physical thing, but compassion and love and empathy and soul. It's our birthright, one of the joys this life offers abundantly to all who will take it.

Some of these "angels" pull people from burning buildings,

donate organs to dying children, or give vast amounts of money to worthy causes. Thankfully, not every day is a "burning building" kind of day! But the opportunity to be an angel in some way does present itself daily. It's a never-ending opportunity.

You know those people who have mastered the art of everyday angel blessings. They have a peace and joy and serenity about them that shows. They live their lives and make their choices by reaching out to others first, in patience and acceptance, not judgment. They make mistakes, but they know how to correct them. They are always looking forward, not back. They see the best, take it, and leave the rest behind.

On a very basic level, we are all alike—in need of affirmation and acceptance, desiring peace and joy and someone to help us when we're down. We want to see goodness in the humanity around us and believe that people do care. We want to be touched by others with that spirit of giving that defines the everyday angel. We need to both give and receive.

We can be the kind of "attendant spirits" that others need if we recognize and seize those opportunities that God puts before us. We can reach out, spiritual being to spiritual being, every day, in small ways, passing on time and thoughtfulness, compassion and strength. You don't have to have wings or a halo!

Being an everyday angel isn't hard, time-consuming, or

expensive. It often takes just a minute and seems completely insignificant. It's a matter of giving what you have and listening with your heart. It requires no advanced degree, but it does take intuition and attention. The rewards are not mantelpieces or public recognition—they are far greater, and you'll reap surprising benefits long after your actions are over. Give, and it will come back to you.

God didn't breathe life and spirit into you only to have you become a doctor or teacher, artist or singer, mom or dad. He's also given you an "attendant spirit" to do the real job we all have here every day—to reach out to others, to meet needs and touch hearts, to be everyday angels.

CHAPTER 2

How to Be an Everyday Angel

Do you know how to be an angel? I think that God told us all how, naturally. Some people are just more practiced at it than others. You know who they are—those people who always seem to know the right thing to do or say. They're always the same: calm and secure, giving and thoughtful. They're not perfect or immune from pain. They're still very human, but their attendant spirit is as visible as the color of their eyes. They know how to be everyday angels. They never miss a chance.

Recognize the opportunity
Rarely does the angel opportunity knock briskly on your heart and say, "Here I am." But it might, if you'll just learn to listen. Sometimes the opportunities may seem unusual or inconvenient, but you'll know when it's right. The mother in the following story knew it instinctively.

A young girl of thirteen or fourteen wasn't sleepy, though

it was late at night. She doesn't remember how it started, and she probably didn't think much of it at the time, but now she recalls it often.

She loved mushrooms—anything with a mushroom on it was an instant favorite, especially that printed contact paper her mother had found. It was covered with tiny pictures of mushrooms, the prettiest ones she'd ever seen. She loved them, and she wanted them everywhere.

Was it her idea or her mother's? She doesn't remember, but that night, until well past her bedtime, she and her mom sat cross-legged on her bed and cut out hundreds of the mushrooms from the contact paper. They carefully peeled off the backing and decorated the entire headboard and footboard of her bed.

Her mother never complained or asked how she'd remove them when she grew tired of mushrooms. The girl doesn't recall their conversation, but she remembers sitting there, talking and laughing with her mother, for hours into the night. She knows that the angel that appeared to her that night was very human, very familiar, and very loved.

Reach out to those who serve you
The Sunday school teacher was feeling overwhelmed as Christmastime approached. Pressures from home, family,

job, and church were weighing on her mind. She had very little help. On the Sunday before Christmas, when her class of four year olds would be expecting a special treat, she was totally unprepared. She grabbed her lesson materials and hurried to church, her mind and body too tired to plan the big party she always had for the children.

When one of her little charges came through the door, he was followed by his mom. The mom didn't contribute a lot to the class, and she and the teacher weren't especially close. But for some reason that day, the mom provided what the teacher couldn't. She had made cupcakes and party bags for all the children, brought plates and napkins, and offered to stay and help.

"You're a godsend." The teacher almost cried. An angel had walked into her classroom that day, an "attendant spirit" of human flesh and bone sent by God, just like the teacher said.

See the big picture

Sometimes it's hard to be angelic to those we distrust or dislike. Even if the opportunity comes with fireworks and trumpets, we're inclined to ignore it and invest our energies elsewhere. But the spiritual part of you will always look for the bigger picture, that aerial view above the pettiness and ego. Follow it.

A mother was enjoying Mother's Day with her two sons.

She was a good mother, and the boys were blessed to have her. But they had a stepmother, too, who loved them very much. Did the children mention their stepmother that day, or did their mother? It doesn't matter.

About midafternoon, they went to the stepmother's house. The boys each took her a plant that she could place in her flower garden. They hugged her and told her they loved her. They were only there a minute. The mother and step-mother never talked, but they didn't have to.

The mother didn't take the boys there out of obligation or some misguided effort to score points. She was simply an earthly angel that day. The stepmother knew it, and they were both blessed.

Realize you're not alone

We're proud of our differences these days. We like doing things our own way, but deep down we're all very much alike—and we all need help from time to time. The needs vary, but the response doesn't have to. Reach out with your heart. You may not be able to save an entire city, but you can be an angel to one person at a time, somehow, everyday.

A newspaper story told of a woman in a county south of town. She was in her late thirties, but she looked much older. She had many health problems. Her two teenage sons had each been diagnosed with incurable diseases. She was raising her daughter's son—though she hadn't even seen her daughter since the boy was born six years earlier. She couldn't work, and she was about to be evicted from her apartment.

The day the story ran, a gentleman appeared at the apartment complex and anonymously paid that month's rent. Another person appeared to pay the next month's rent. Donations made to a bank account covered the cost of the medicine she and her sons needed. The everyday angels had appeared. The anonymous "attendant spirits" were alive and well here on earth, practicing what they had learned. Let no one doubt them. Let them multiply.

CHAPTER 3

Be an Everyday Angel to Your Spouse

In this hurry-up world, the person we're closest to is sometimes the easiest one to forget. When that happens, it's a loss for both you and your spouse. Take a few minutes each day to grasp the angel opportunities your marriage presents, and you'll both be blessed.

The suggestions here are simple. Few require much time or money. All of them are worthwhile. Your own unique situation may offer many opportunities not listed here. Whatever you do, seize the moment, and be an angel to your spouse.

1. Put a short note in your spouse's lunch bag or briefcase. It doesn't have to be long or involved. A simple "I love you, and I appreciate you" is priceless.

15

2. When you see your spouse getting ready for a special evening, take the time to say, "You look great." Give your undivided attention for just a moment—really watching him or her with a look that says, "I noticed you. I'm proud of you." It'll do wonders.

3. If you're independently wealthy, this suggestion may not apply to you! If not. . .think of what your spouse wants but can't afford—that big something that he talks about all the time. Save up for it a little at a time, even if it takes months. When you've got the money saved, surprise him. Your love and thoughtfulness will mean more than the item itself.

4. Before a special show or the big game, clean the television screen.

5. Wash and clean out your spouse's car. Empty all the trash, wash the floor mats, clean the windows. Leave a favorite piece of candy in the console.

6. The next time you drive your spouse's car, fill the gas tank before you bring it back.

7. Check out the magazines devoted to your spouse's hobby or favorite pastime. Order him or her a surprise subscription, or pick up the latest book about the subject. It doesn't cost much, and it says that you care enough to learn what your lover cares about.

8. Who does what around your house? The division of labor is usually fairly predictable, and we all have chores we dislike. Do one of your spouse's chores each week. It'll be a welcomed surprise.

9. Encourage your spouse to try something new—to take that class, learn some new skill, try a new profession. Help research the topic. Borrow books or videos from the library. Find some web sites and request information. People can do more than they think they can when someone they love is encouraging them. Keep saying, "I believe in you."

10. Try your spouse's sport, even if you have absolutely no interest in it. Ask questions and learn—everything has a vocabulary and life of its own. Show your spouse that you respect his or her interests.

11. Fill a "goody basket" for your spouse to carry to work. The basket can be fancy or a paper sack—it doesn't really matter. Fill it with favorite candies, a pack of gum, note paper, one of those pens he likes so much, batteries, a tiny clock, a funny joke, a small framed snapshot of a time she enjoyed. . . . You get the idea. Everything in there will say, "I listen to you. I know what you like."

12. Learn when to bite your tongue. Sometimes it just won't help a thing to say what you think, and it may only make the situation worse. If you can't help matters with your comments, keep the comments to yourself. Now that is truly angelic!

13. Everybody loves lists. Write one for your spouse. Begin each item with "I love you because. . ." or "I remember when we. . ." It will be a treasured keepsake.

14. Make a screen saver for your spouse. Even if you can't draw, use your computer's paint program and fashion a simple heart with the message, "I

love you." Or be more elaborate by adding clip art or photos. It doesn't have to win a blue ribbon, but you can bet it will be prized beyond the works of all the masters.

15. Write a letter to your spouse, saying what you would tell him if you never saw him again. Put it in a sealed envelope in a safe deposit box and tell him to open it if something happens to you. Say everything you need to say in the letter. Do your best to say it to him every day, too.

16. Remember that whatever you're fighting over is far less important than your marriage. Keep the proper perspective—just how big is the crisis and what kind of day do you want tomorrow to be? Compromise. End the fight.

17. If your spouse has trouble remembering dates or times, write him or her notes and reminders. Stick them in the car, or the lunch bag, or on the bathroom mirror. Send an E-mail reminder or leave a message on the answering machine.

18. Make his or her outside work a little more pleasant. Show up with a cold drink in the summer and a warm drink in the winter. The gesture may seem tiny, but it shows you're paying attention.

19. Hold her hand in public. Make those subtle advances that say, "I love you and I want everyone here to know it."

20. Wash her glasses or sunglasses.

21. Listen when your spouse talks. Turn off the television or put down the newspaper—and don't complain about being interrupted. Focus on what he or she is saying. Pay attention and remember the details.

22. Every time one of you leaves the house, say, "I love you." Don't forget.

CHAPTER 4

Be an Everyday Angel
to Your Children

It's true that children generally become what they see. They will see how to become everyday angels when they see you reaching out to others—when they witness it every day. They will know how an angel's touch feels when it comes from you to them. They will know its value, and they will learn to pass it on. You may have to sandwich those angelic opportunities with your children in between book reports and bubble baths, but make no mistake—those brief, sometimes mundane moments are as nourishing and necessary as dinner.

23. Write a letter to your child for her birthday. It doesn't need to be long and sentimental. Use your child's age in the letter. If it's a tenth birthday, for example, write ten things you like about her.

24. Make your child a "memory box." It can be as simple or elaborate as you choose. Use souvenirs from a special event to capture a day he'll want to remember over and over again. You can make as many memory boxes as your child wants—it's a great way to build a tradition.

25. Admit to your kids that you have fears. Sometimes, kids think that parents don't understand fears, or they feel embarrassed about being afraid. Show them that you are afraid sometimes, too.

26. Praise all of your child's efforts when he's trying to master a new skill. Everybody can perform better with a little encouragement. To simply say, "I can see you're trying hard and making progress," shows him that you've noticed. He knows you're in his corner when it gets tough.

27. Write your child a story. Make your son or daughter the star, and build the story around what he or she likes to do. Take a walk and tell the story. Maybe together you can illustrate it. They won't be expecting Mark Twain, so don't

think your story won't be good enough. It will be, and rest assured that it will become their very favorite.

28. Write your teen a story. This time, put him in that career he's been dreaming of. Include some hobbies or favorite places. Bind the story in a folder or even just staple it down the side. It doesn't matter. It will be a keepsake your teen will treasure, even if he doesn't say so!

29. Let your kids play outside in the rain. Have dry clothes and towels ready when they're done. Take their picture.

30. Always take the time to notice the sunrise and sunset, the autumn leaves, a rainbow. Stop what you're doing and get your children and just look. Quietly, for a few moments, let them see that you are in awe of God's handiwork. They will learn to appreciate the wonders of nature and want to share the beauty with others, just like you've done with them.

31. Always listen when your children want to talk, especially the older they get. Never underestimate the importance of what appears to be a meaningless conversation. Your attention is the goal. Listen—and don't interrupt.

32. Rake a pile of leaves for your child to jump in.

33. Do it again.

34. If your children drop their shoes in a mud room, bring them inside before school to get warm when the weather outside is cold.

35. Surprise your child with a new gadget for school. It doesn't have to be expensive. Simply hide it in her backpack with a card attached that says you're always thinking of her.

36. Put an extra piece of candy in his lunchbox—or quarters for a special treat.

37. Children's furniture gets abused fast, but it doesn't have to look like it belongs in the trash. Let them

choose some fabric, maybe a favorite character print, and cover the furniture with it. Just staple-gun it in place. They'll love it.

38. Make sock puppets. Give the puppets names and let them go to the grocery story or the doctor's office. It only takes a little time and imagination.

39. Children love the very things you usually want to throw out. Collect some discarded craft or hobby items and put them in a special "mystery box." Give the box to your children in a special way.

40. Play in the "mystery box" with them.

41. Put fresh flowers in your child's room. We don't often think of giving flowers to children, but perhaps we should. Flowers say, "I'm thinking of you. You're special to me."

42. Always tell your child you're proud of him when you catch him being good. It's so easy to correct bad behavior, but it's just as important to recognize and appreciate good behavior. When your

child has been helpful or compassionate or generous, tell him that you noticed. Be sure that he understands your pride and appreciation.

43. If your child has to miss her favorite program, videotape it for her as a surprise.

44. When your child is away with grandparents or at camp, send her an "I miss you" card. Children don't get much mail, and anything addressed to them is indeed treasured. Enclose something flat—a bookmark, a page of stickers, a dollar.

45. Read to your children as long as they'll let you. It doesn't have to be the classics, and it doesn't have to be at bedtime. It's just the sound of your voice, unhurried, focused on them.

46. Every time one of you leaves the house, say, "I love you." Don't forget.

CHAPTER 5

Be an Everyday Angel
to Your Family and Friends

Life is full of opportunities to reach out to family and friends
—and not only in the forty-six ways we've already discussed
for spouses and children! The ideas in this chapter will also
apply to your immediate family, but also to the extended family and outside friends who grace your life. You might have
everything in the world—but it amounts to nothing if you don't
share it with those around you. Everything is doubled when
you do. Giving of yourself, in even the tiniest way, says "I care."
The gesture may seem small, but the impact can be great.

47. Share a happy memory with a friend. Sometimes
    the joy of the past can offer great promise for the
    future. Let your friend know that you remember

and cherish your times together, that you value your friendship.

48. Whenever you visit a friend with a baby, bring a box of diapers—even a small one will do.

49. Give a friend a small flower or plant clipping for her office. Pot it in an old coffee cup that she's admired or will remember. Deliver it.

50. Send E-mail cards to your family and friends with Internet access. The cards are free and easy—and they say, "I'm thinking of you." Send special occasion cards, silly occasion cards, and no occasion cards. They'll love them all.

51. Clip magazine or newspaper articles that your friends or family members would like to read. Drop them in the mail. People still love snail mail, too.

52. Prepare a casserole for a friend who's sick or overworked. Put it in a throw-away pan.

53. Put fresh pillowcases on the beds between sheet-changing days.

54. Drop some ice cubes in your pet's water bowl during hot summer days. In the winter, keep a pan of water near his bed.

55. Let your present on that special day—Mother's Day, Father's Day, Grandparents' Day, a friend's birthday—be a handwritten letter. Tell the person what you appreciate about him or her. Relate your favorite memory. Your words will be a cherished gift.

56. Place a little money, maybe five or ten dollars, where someone who needs it will find it. Proclaim the "finders keepers" rule.

57. Let someone tell you a story that he's told a thousand times before. Don't complain.

58. Buy a box of Christmas cards and stamps for an elderly friend or family member. Help her address them.

59. Take at least five minutes a day to play outside with your pet. Give him your undivided attention.

60. Make a pitcher of homemade lemonade for your family.

61. Take a tray of snacks to your job. If you don't bake, that's all right. Goodies of any kind are always appreciated.

62. Leave a "Have a happy day" card and a treat for your mail carrier, on any old, regular day.

63. Leave a "Have a happy day" card and a treat for your newspaper carrier, on any old, regular day.

64. Your talents are God-given and meant to be shared, even if you think those talents are minimal. Find an old frame and paint a picture for someone special. It doesn't matter what it is or how good of an artist you are. Just paint something the person likes, frame it yourself, and give it with love. It will say, "You mean a lot to me."

65. Offer whatever "fix-it" talents you have to your friends. Can you sew? Repair a piece of clothing for them. Can you make the error messages on their computer go away? The opportunities are always there to help.

66. Maybe you have supplies that you don't need anymore, for hobbies you no longer pursue. Donate those supplies to a daycare class or church group.

67. From those talents that you still pursue, donate pieces of your work to your community, your child's school, or a charitable organization's auction.

68. Teach someone else how to do whatever it is that you do. Are you a skilled carpenter? A master chess player? A gourmet cook? Share what you know with others. You'll all learn.

69. Clean up after yourself, at home and work and play. There is no reason why someone else should have to do it for you.

70. Take a couple of hours and visit your oldest relative. Take her shopping. Do some yard work or laundry. Listen to her stories.

71. Keep a list of items your friends collect. Shop garage sales and flea markets for inexpensive items on the list. When you've collected enough, put them in a "thinking of you" basket—just because.

72. Remind a troubled friend or family member that you're available. Some people find it hard to ask for help and don't want to impose. Send a card that says, "I'm always here for you." Call the next day.

73. Remember others' special days—the first day of a new job, the first day of school, whatever. Send a note of good wishes or call with a quick, "You'll do great!"

74. Accept your friends and family members exactly as they are. Focus on their good qualities. Ask for their opinions.

75. When your friend or family member experiences a great success, share in the joy with her. Be proud of her accomplishment and make it a special day for her. Everyday angels are just as important in times of joy as in times of sadness!

76. Be a trusted friend. Keep secrets and don't betray confidences.

77. Run a library. Share your special books with special people and tell them why. If you've scribbled notes in the margins, that's even better.

78. Only give the advice that is asked of you. Unsolicited advice is usually unwelcome. Listen attentively. Don't correct, interrupt, argue, or judge. Just listen. It's always the best place to start.

79. Put a photo album together, or even just a photo collage in a small frame, to commemorate a special relationship or a special time. Give it to your friend as soon as you're done. Don't wait for a special occasion.

80. When your friend admires something of yours, consider giving it to her. You won't be without it—it'll still be a piece of the story that you both share, just living in a new home.

81. Resist the urge to say, "I told you so."

82. Keep your promises. Do your very best to deliver even more than you promised.

83. Forgive. Then forget.

Chapter 6

Be an Everyday Angel, Anonymously

Normally, it's easy and fun to be an everyday angel for the people we love. It just seems natural. It may seem a little less natural to reach out to those people we don't know or ones we may never see again. But it's just as needed.

84. When someone is especially friendly or helpful to you while doing her job, express your thanks and send a short note to her supervisor. People like that make our day-to-day trials so much easier to handle.

85. There are needs to be filled all around us. If you can afford it, anonymously put some money— even a small amount—in someone's bank account.

86. Let someone cut in front of you in the check-out line.

87. Volunteer at the agency of your choice. If you don't have the time to visit a nursing home or deliver meals, you may be able to pick up supplies, run an errand, or stuff envelopes.

88. Clean up the sanctuary of your church between Sunday night and Wednesday night. Just make a quick trip to pick up trash and return books to the proper places. Dash in and out without being seen!

89. Send a gift basket of goodies or supplies to your doctor's office or your hairdresser. Include a note that just says, "You're appreciated!"

90. "Adopt" a class at a preschool or daycare center. Determine the children's birthdays and send a little gift from "a secret friend" on each child's special day.

91. Secretly plant some flowers for a non-gardening friend.

92. When your neighbor's away, mow his lawn.

93. Create some "Appreciation Day" cards for your local police or fire department. Send the cards with a box of candy.

94. Pay attention to the people you work with, attend church with, or see elsewhere regularly. Is there something that they need and can't afford? If you can afford to buy what they need, do it, but don't let them know where it came from.

95. Whatever your talents are, use them to touch others. Create or build what you can. Give the items away to people you don't know.

96. Prepay for gas or groceries for someone in need. Any amount will be appreciated.

97. Be a courteous driver.

98. Make the best of any bad situation. If the line is long, make a friend. If the waitress is new, be patient and forgiving. When someone makes a mistake, remember that we all do.

99. Give people the benefit of the doubt. Before you retaliate for bad service or rude comments, consider the possible causes. Maybe the person isn't well. Maybe he has more problems than you do. Maybe he could use a friend. Or an angel. . .

CHAPTER 7

Your Record of Everyday Angels—
When Angels Come to You

100. Always appreciate everything that is done for you, even the minor, day-to-day routine things, because they add up to something much bigger. Always remember to say "thank you."

Now it's time to make a different list. The everyday angels are truly everywhere, thank God. They will touch your life as you touch others. They will bring you joy and encouragement, compassion and hope.

Take the time to recognize these everyday angel visits. God has surely sent them to you when you've needed them.

He has guided your family, your friends, and even strangers to meet your needs. He has done it in the past when you've not even realized it. He will continue to do it in the future when you need it most.

You will be pleasantly surprised by some of these angels. They will come when you feel alone, when you doubt their existence, when you're lost and afraid. They will appear, not in robes of white or descending on clouds, but in the mortal flesh that we all share. Their mission, though, is no less spiritual.

The everyday angels will appear because you need them, plain and simple. They will be your attendant servants. Be grateful for them. Thank God for them.